21 Days of Menial Thoughts

Alexis Collier

BookLeaf Publishing

Presentation by *BookLeaf Publishing*

Web: www.bookleafpub.com

E-mail: info@bookleafpub.com

ISBN: 9789357211802

First edition 2023

DEDICATION

To mum & dad, it was about time I listened to you and followed some dreams.

PREFACE

'Poetry is just the evidence of life. If your life is burning well, poetry is just the ash.'
- Leonard Cohen

Day One: Bread Is My Religion

Bread is my religion.
I pray to it.
I make a declaration of love daily.
I wonder what Bread is thinking.
What is it thinking?

Bread can come in so many forms;
Accessible to all.
Now even gluten-free!
Bread gives life and sustains the soul,
(too much Bread can kill you though
— it bringeth and taketh).

Bread is the perfect partner.
It pairs with cheese,
Condiments and charcuterie.
Bread goes with more Bread.
What is not to love?

Bread is poetry in one's mouth.
The moist, soft flesh falls apart.
Butter arouses when it's upon Bread.
Bread is the beginning of everything.

Bread was the start of civilisation.

Human history is based on Bread.
The price of Bread explains economies.
Bread is my religion.

But Bread does not ask for forgiveness.
Bread does not ask for death;
Nor hate, nor rage, nor murder in its name.
Bread is pure; Bread is for all.

Bread will surely kill me.
It makes my belly rotund.
Bread is my religion.
Like all religions, it will make me disappear.
Probably with a heart attack.
I do not trust those who dislike Bread.

Alas! Bread is my religion.
Perhaps not too different to the others.

Day Two: All Problems Can Be Solved With Negronis

Negronis are like a cool hug from friends,
Followed by a slap* in the face.
What were you thinking? It would say.
When you decided a fringe would look neat.

Negronis are the therapist after a long day,
Followed by a slap in the face.
"Everyone is the worst, and I hate them all,"
Negroni agrees; Negroni always agrees.

Negronis are where problems disappear like ice,
Followed by a slap in the face.
They make you forget your problems,
Just for a little while.

Negronis are the best way to die;
They're blood-red bitter, classically dramatic
and best enjoyed with friends.
What better way to die?
Except…
…followed by a slap in the face.

*No people or Negronis were harmed in the making of this poem. Therefore, all slaps should be read as symbolic.

Day Three: Broken

My heart was bruised
The easy intimacy was all but gone
Like shards hitting my fingertips

You were taken too soon
A thousand paper cuts rupture your face
Your purpose now obsolete

Your name will be forgotten to time
Did you have a name?
You were but an innocent

I shall replace you, dear friend
It won't take long, I suppose
"Just thirty pieces of gold"
Broken Screen Protector: Now Sold

Day Four: i just want to know how they get up there

dusty unruly writing,
tortured autograph,
defaced freeway street signs,
how high they travelled to sign you,
how high! and why?

Day Five: Writer's Block

I stare at a blank page.
Write, write, write;
my hand does not move.
Write, write, write;
blasphemous hand betrays me.

Wave at a friend; it waves.
Eat ten too-many chocolate digestives?
It raises quickly to my ill-gotten mouth.
My hand works, you see?

Time moves not a minute,
Write, write, write;
nothing.
Write, write, write;
again this hand betrays me.

But then it says one thing,
"write what you fool?
Show purpose, and the writing will begin.
You do not wish for words as much as
digestives."

Day Six: Shower Thoughts

Who called the earth, earth?
Why do I start breathing weirdly when I think about breathing?
The funny bone is not funny.
Just some shower thoughts.

Permanent markers are rarely permanent.
Why is the K silent in 'know'?
Why don't umbrellas have handles on the side?
Just some shower thoughts.

Why is the four-leaf clover lucky?
When genetic deformity is rarely seen as so.
How can you patent a colour, like Tiffany & Co.?
Just some shower thoughts.

Love is patient. Love is kind.
Why do they forget that part?
Why do my toes need hair?
Just some shower thoughts.

Somewhere in the world, your dream life is being lived,
and they hate it.

Be a little kinder in yours.
Just some shower thoughts.

Day Seven: A Love Affair

Federico my love,
how you tease me so!

Federico my love,
how much adulation can I show?

Federico my darling,
my heart is at a low.

Federico my darling,
when your thoughts I do not know.

Federico my sweet,
you're pissing me off, a lot!

Federico my sweet,
with that goddamn top knot.

Federico you ass,
caught red-handed in her pants.

Federico you ass,
what I get for dating on tinder, here endeth my rants.

Day Eight: The Only Two Constants: Death & Taxes

In death, you are alone, said she,
Alas! I have a plan, you'll see.

I'll die with a book in the palms of my hands,
And thus I'll expire with friends in new lands.

Alone I won't be, whilst sailing the seas,
With Ishmael, Hook and Doctor Livsey!

Day Nine: Poetry Isn't Hard…

Wondering heart and lonely lion,
The truth is dark when feeling is iron,
When cur-sed saw a brand-new world,
I hath forgiven him in recluse shirts.

Never did I hasten a wild sown oat,
Into his heart the strings of church,
Mind the tide the ships may fall,
Hasten unto him doth penny wore.

'Life is cursed', said the ole beggar long ago,
Find the truth in his lips and then grow,
Listen to the tide and begin again,
This poem makes no sense, jokes on you, my friend.

Written on a toilet break in one go,
leaving the brain to ramble to-and-fro.

Day Ten: 21 Reasons Why*

He cuts his spaghetti
He's salty, incredibly petty
He said he works 'too hard'
Only has 40 hours on his punch card
20 reasons why I hate this lard

He thinks the world owes him something
Life owes him one thing…nothing
He wanders without a plan
Confused why his life is a trash can
20 reasons why I loathe this man

He plays at love like some harlot
Breaking hearts with an 'A' of scarlet
It's all a game if it's someone else's wife
He's okay if it's only them in strife
20 reasons why I resent his life

He wants all the riches and the gold
But unwilling to gamble three-fold
He likes them deaf, blind and dumb
It is his succinct 'rule of thumb'
20 reasons why I pity this scum

I may have only got to eight

Reasons as to why I hate
So here's some more for your plate
He's a fraud; causes discord; behaves like some lord; he's just so overboard. He spends what he can't afford; drinks lemonade and Chambord; never thinks about people he's ignored; plays his friends like a chessboard; always eats the most on a cheeseboard; i'm wondering why he's not abhorred, just like a drug lord; always listens like he's blithely bored,
20 reasons why my hatred soared

One reason why my contempt is all moot
He's my best mate's boyfriend; there's nothing I can refute; now,
21 reasons why I hate this rapacious brute

*thank god she dumped him

Day Eleven: What Life is Like as a Successful Adult

Hark! Fark!
Stubbed my toe in the dark

Is there anything worse?
Shout to the heavens in a curse

Hark! Fark!
No toilet paper in the dark

I stumble to the cupboard,
Looking like Old Mother Hubbard

Hark! Fark!
I forgot to buy lavatorial roll,
But how will I wipe my own asshole?

Day Twelve: What Life is Like as a Successful Adult Pt II

She looked at me,
Then she looked away,
The smile seemed to say, ‘hello,’
or perhaps, a ‘good day!’

Perchance I imagined it,
What friends we could be.
It’s tough making friends,
Past the age of seventeen.

Alone I walk home,
To my empty house of one,
This is why people buy dogs,
An invention for the lonesome.

She looked at me, I’m sure,
I should have said hi, I implored.
I stand at my mirror to clear my headspace,
Well, blast! That’s bloody ink on my face!

Day Thirteen: what do you want for dinner?

what do you want for dinner?

- i don’t know -

what do you feel like?

- anything -

what about Indian?

- anything, but Indian -

well not ‘anything’ then

- anything -

you choose then

- i’m happy with your choice -

clearly not though

[he side-eyes me]

this might lead to divorce
friendships might end
wars will ravage lands
people will surely starve
the choices never end
'tis the hardest part of being an adult
choosing dinner every day
…until you die

Day Fourteen: The Power of No

Nope, never, nay-nay.
So many ways to say, not today, no way!
They may say, saying yes, is a sign of less stress.
They might call me crappy, but I will die happy;
When I deftly said no and not yes!

Day Fifteen: Teeny Tiny Towels

Hotel towels
Small, teeny
'le petite'
Unable to fit around 'double d's'

Sheet fitted tightly
An arm wrestle
Unleash yourself for me
I must sleep
I must

Mini fridge
Not cold, just cool
Unable to fit a bottle of water
Is it on? Is it waiting?
What use are you?

Night lights burn bright
It's for reading
No, it's for torture
The Gestapo is back
One can't gently fall asleep
"Where were you on the 19th, comrade?"

Tiny teeny towels
36 channels of static
Power points behind beds
193 countries
Two observer states
Eleven sovereign states
So many laws
So many cultures
But all hotels speak the same language

Day Sixteen: i mourn you

i mourn you
truly mourn you
i have my freedom
my life is mine to own again
i am grateful
but that closeness to another
you were my person
now you're gone
and i mourn you

here and there I flutter
eating soup dumplings
you come to me
uninvited in my mind
smirking beneath ruby hair

i will mourn you until i die
i'm happy you're with her
happy, truly
but i mourn you
two truths exist
sometimes i wish you were here
with chopsticks
also, these dumplings are shit

Day Seventeen: Sugar

Communal sugar, you dare me,
Dare the hand that touches thine lid.
When were you last wiped?
When did you feel the spray?

Communal sugar upon tables,
Nestled between salt and pepper.
How many teaspoons have dug you?
How many secrets have you heard?

Communal sugar, you deceive us,
Glass jar with a perfect lid.
How much is a sachet to a teaspoon?
Is it half? Is it heaped? Or two?

Not all spoons are created 'Equal',
'Communal Sugar Pt. II', coming soon, the
sequel.

Day Eighteen: Salty Treats

No. Stop.
'I have no control when it comes to salty snacks',
Said the Negroni drinker to the barkeeper.

No. Stop.
'Where art thou snacks?'
Costco pretzels, you ruin me,
Loathsome things;
Delightful treats.

Dead. Here she lies.
From salt.
Delicious salt.

Day Nineteen: tonight I am lonely

it’s lonely being strong.
as I walk the streets alone.
it’s freeing, but it’s hard.
butterflies in shards.

tonight i am lonely.
like the dot upon the i.
night will pass like spring,
in the morning i will sing.

they think i don’t have feelings,
those girls who aren’t 'alone',
their tonight won’t pass in flings,
but mine will pass in spring.

Day Twenty: uncomfortably comfy

the sheets aren't fresh
clothes so restrictive
the light is on
socks are tight
but lordy, I'm so uncomfortably comfy

i won't get up just yet
a little while longer in bed
my face is unwashed
why did i lie down, just then?
oh lord, so uncomfortably comfy

i will wake with a crick in my neck
surely it's reason to get up then?
my pants are getting tighter
something is crawling in my bed…
but damn it, i'm so uncomfortably comfy

i open my phone
yep, i'm not moving then
is that a spider i see sleuthing?
meh, i'll be uncomfortably comfy instead

Day Twenty-One: Close Me Up

The light kiss of the last page
A closed book
Finished
Complete
A drug

Internal rewards of completion
Better than sex
-- Almost
No, better

The leaves have been touched
Turned
Bristled between fingers
Your eyes scanned, roamed

Is there anything more joyful than reading?
-- Yes, sex
Apart from that
-- Food
Okay, sex, food, then reading

Oh, I would die happy
Sex, food and reading

For sex to be with someone I loved
For food to not have calories
For reading to take you to new worlds

For now, I will have to make do with one
I'll let you guess which, for fun

www.ingramcontent.com/pod-product-compliance
Lightning Source LLC
Chambersburg PA
CBHW051751130826
49812CB00033B/1100
9789357211802